Steggy
A True Story

Marty Gower Cole

To Mom
Vera Katherine McCombs Gower
1900-2000
who always wanted me to write something

and to Walter Eugene
who has always and forever been there for me

and to Alex
wherever you are

Steggy
A True Story

It has been said that dinosaurs had very small brains. That was not always the case, however. I was a dinosaur and I had a deep capacity for understanding. My memory was quite remarkable. Why, I could even remember my creation …

Creation

In Faye Swartzendrover's fifth grade classroom the children were busy tearing inch-wide strips of the *Fort Dodge Messenger*, oblivious to the printed news stories, dipping the strips into pots of gooey white paste, smoothing them flat between thumb and forefinger and letting the gloppy white excess dribble back into the pot. Paste caked on knuckles and wrists and when dry, peeled off in a grotesquely delightful fashion. Ten-year-old Martha Jane did her best to flip two long braids behind her as she worked, keeping the tassel ends out of the paste. Over and over she wound strip after strip onto my slender newspaper frame, ridiculously slender for a Stegosaurus, I must say. With care she formed the triangular plates along the length of my back-bone and long sweeping tail. When finished, I measured a full 30 inches long and

a proud 10 inches high to the tips of my magnificent plates. The process took more than a week because one day's work had to dry before new layers could be applied. Finally, Martha Jane placed me in the crowd of Brontosauruses, Tyrannosauruses, and other Jurassic friends on the classroom's back table to dry for several days. Once our prehistoric menagerie was dry, the pots of primary poster paint came out of the supply cupboard and the magic began. I turned a lovely soft green; decorative red lines and white dots graced each of my triangular plates and encircled my stumpy feet. Two bright yellow marble eyes, with small black dots for pupils, gave me an alert intelligent look. My mouth was crimson and painted in a wobbly smile.

Coming Home

At the completion of the fifth grade dinosaur project, Martha Jane carried me through the town to my new home. It was a large square brick house with screened porches on two levels which faced the morning sun and was located at the end of a dead end street. Woods sloped down from the house to the south; two Russian olive trees with low curved limbs ideal for climbing graced the end of the street. This wood of bur oak, elm, and maple which shaded Virginia bluebells, May apples, honeysuckle and wild ginger was called "The Hill" by the family. The children were not to go down the hill alone;

it was true that occasionally, though rarely, hobos who hopped off the freight trains two small valleys below, wandered up the hill to the house looking for handouts.

I wasn't the only animal in the house. There was a nice little dog they called Blackie who had appeared one day at the door and stayed. For a number of months there was a crow named Jet who would settle on the windowsill outside the room where most of the family members were gathered. Like the children and the dog, Jet came home whenever the mother stood outside and whistled her sliding two-note signal.

The curious sight of two children, a dog, and a large black bird hurrying home to dinner in response to a mother's whistle amazed the neighbors. There were orphaned baby rabbits for a time who tended to escape from their box into the labyrinth of basement rooms.

Of course there were the other animals as well, rather like me. Among them were an oddly zebra-like dinosaur fashioned by Walter Eugene when he was in Miss Swartzendrover's class,

a panda stuffed with straw, an orange and white gingham dog, a brown teddy bear with a jingle bell in one ear, a Steiff lion, and his small tiger companion.

The dolls were another group of permanent residents. Ginnie, Sally and Billy were bald and had eyes that opened and closed; Nancy, a newcomer with hair that could be combed, tended to be a bit uppity. The Raggedy Anns were weary from so much loving, and the patchwork clown's satin knees were worn thin.

The Closet

Years passed. The children grew up, married, and established families of their own. I ended up on a high shelf in the closet of an upstairs bedroom. My life became quiet but not altogether lonely; the old straw-filled panda lived in the same closet as did a box of small animals, some made of glass, others of china or wood, bronze or plastic, collected over the years from grandparents, museum shops and cereal boxes. Having sent in three Wheaties box tops and a dime, Martha Jane

had a Captain Midnight secret decoder. Walter Eugene was proud of his Tom Mix plastic arrowhead with magnifying glass and whistle, which only cost four cardboard panels from Wheat Chex boxes.

There were books and magazines on shelves in my closet. I found myself in the company of some little Peppers and Moffats, a skin horse and his soft rabbit friend, Pooh, Dr. Dolittle, a little prince and his rose, the stallion Midnight and Michael, Nancy Drew and the Brownie Scouts. Honestly, I could recite all those stories if you asked me. Those Peppers and Moffats were a bit unrealistic and I felt that the rabbit of velveteen was a wee bit too sentimental for this old dinosaur. However, I would come to feel differently later, as you will see.

But *The Chestry Oak*! Now there's a story! War, evil, honor, tradition, drama, joy, love of homeland, love of family, and throughout, the love between a small boy and the dangerous stallion Midnight. And I nearly fell off my shelf, laughing, when I heard a small child talk about "Pinnie-the-Wooh." I also knew, cover by cover, the wonderful scenes that wrapped around the *Jack and Jill* magazines of the 1940s.

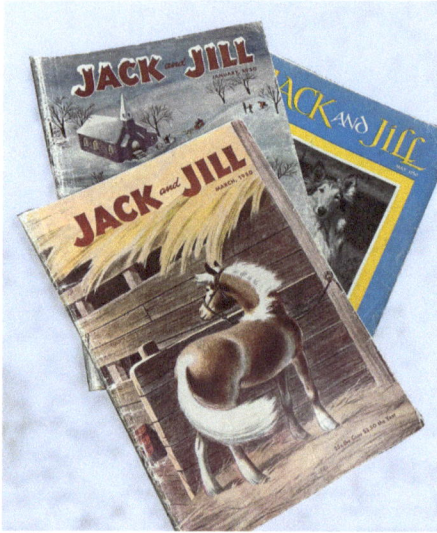

At Christmas, the house filled with people and stirred with old memories brought to life by a sense of nostalgia and love of tradition. Down from the dormer storage closets came the glass ornaments and bubble lights. The electric train was hauled out and set up on its figure-eight course in the third floor playroom, to carry Christmas ribbon candy and peanuts in its hopper cars. Sometimes I would be brought out from my shelf, admired and chuckled over. "Who else would save a 36-year-old papier-mâché dinosaur?" they would say, smiling at Martha Jane. *Well, who wouldn't,* I thought, feeling suddenly vulnerable.

Moving

Parents became grandparents and children, parents. The grandparents slept in the bedroom just outside my shelf in the lovely old walnut bed that had

belonged to the grandfather's Aunt Anna. I could hear the grandmother and grandfather getting ready for bed, settling in under Aunt Maude's hand-stitched quilt. Through the half-open closet door I liked seeing the soft lamp glow on the flower garden quilt, listening to the grandparents' gentle talk and laughter and then their quiet rhythmic snoring.

Then one day the grandfather was gone. The house became even quieter. It was a long time before the grandmother came back upstairs to sleep once again in the old walnut bed outside my closet door. When she did, I felt sturdy and protective as I looked down through the door and watched her sleep; small and delicate and lonely she was in the big bed. I felt important watching over her.

Many years went by. One day a lady came and looked the house over

from top to bottom, inside and out. She peered into everything, from the dormer closets in the playroom down to the dimmest corners of the basement and the garage pegboard covered with tools. When she discovered me on my high shelf, she smiled and said, "Why, that's wonderful! I would say that's real folk art." How I swelled with pride when I heard that. So much so that a couple of my beautiful triangular plates cracked a bit along the ridge of my long back. I was brought out of the closet. Again I was admired fondly with a sense of amazement and nostalgia. I was by this time 40 years old.

Within a few days people began to fill the house. Martha Jane came with her teenage daughter who liked to take long brisk walks in the early mornings, exercise, and take showers. There was a boy about the same age Martha Jane was when she created me. He liked to explore all the corners of the house hoping to find some very old baseball cards or comic books. Martha Jane's husband arrived, and her brother Walter Eugene came with his wife.

Cardboard boxes appeared. Household items began to disappear into them. People reminisced and shared stories that had been told and retold over the years. There was a lot of talk about items "going north." I began to understand that the old house was to be emptied, cleaned, and sold. Walter Eugene and Martha Jane lived with their families in distant towns.

By the weekend there was a large rental truck parked outside, its gaping jaw ready to swallow boxes, tables, chairs, beds, and assorted old treasures. There was discussion about where all the various items were to go. The things assembling in piles were destined for the north, the porch sale, the Goodwill, or the dump. So far I had not been put in any of these categories; I always seemed to be rather apart from things, rather separate. I wondered what north meant and what it would be like to go there.

Walter Eugene noticed me standing off to one side and called out to his sister, "Hey! What about your old Stegosaurus? You *are* taking him with you, aren't you?

If you aren't, then I am. He *is* an old treasure." Martha Jane looked at him steadily, but didn't answer, which I thought strange because she always answered her brother. Perhaps she was thinking about the reality of his kind offer. She knew that however gallant the intention, an aging dinosaur would eventually be relegated to a basement shelf and ultimately end up in a trash can.

By this time I had been out of my closet for a few days and was not feeling too well. I was tired and needed to nap a lot. I suppose I was starting to feel my age. The

life expectancy of papier-mâché dinosaurs crafted by children is often only a matter of months, I had heard, rarely longer than a year or so. My sweeping tail was cracking in several places and gradually a deep gash opened up across my forehead. It was so deep that my face began to droop at an unnatural angle. Martha Jane noticed my wound and carefully mended it with an old tube of airplane cement she found in a cupboard. I felt better, perhaps just for the caring attention I felt under her hands, but my head continued to hurt from time to time.

The big truck pulled out and headed north, as did all but one car. The next few days were fun. Martha Jane moved me from place to place so I could enjoy various vistas. She seemed to study me with particular fondness, though I noticed a strange sadness in her eyes. We spent some time in the tall lilac hedge at Moss Entrance, a favorite childhood hiding place. I tried out different window sills from which I had views of the neighborhood and the wooded ravine. I gazed out the front windows where the filmy curtains swayed in the breeze, inspected the window box of impatiens

and occasionally stood guard over the grandmother while she took an afternoon nap. We
took a walk down the long sidewalk shaded
by immense bur oaks to the little house
perched on the hill behind the brick house.

I spent a couple nights sleeping out on the
screened front porch from where I could look
out on the moonlit lawn through the lace
of Virginia Creeper leaves. Before dozing off
I would watch the fireflies flickering like tiny
winking fairy lights on the summer grass.

One day we had company for lunch. One
of the grandmother's friends brought sand-
wiches and apples and cookies; she knew

there was no food left in the house. The three women invited me to this luncheon party, the last meal shared with a friend in the old brick home. We sat on lawn chairs and on the floor and used a cardboard box for a table.

On the last day people wandered in for a porch sale. If people had seen me, they might have wanted to buy me, so I was carefully set aside on the floor of the empty dining room alongside suitcases and various items yet to be packed, safely closed off from view behind the sliding oak pocket doors. Several people liked the way the old house looked with all the

gleaming oak floors and shining woodwork. Some asked if they could look around all the rooms. Then the grandmother would shyly but proudly show them the photo album of the house with all the furniture and oriental rugs still in place and say quietly, "Look. This is what my home looked like just a week ago." To those interested, Martha Jane would show the back vestibule and pantry and explain how the iceman used to put blocks of ice into the old oak icebox.

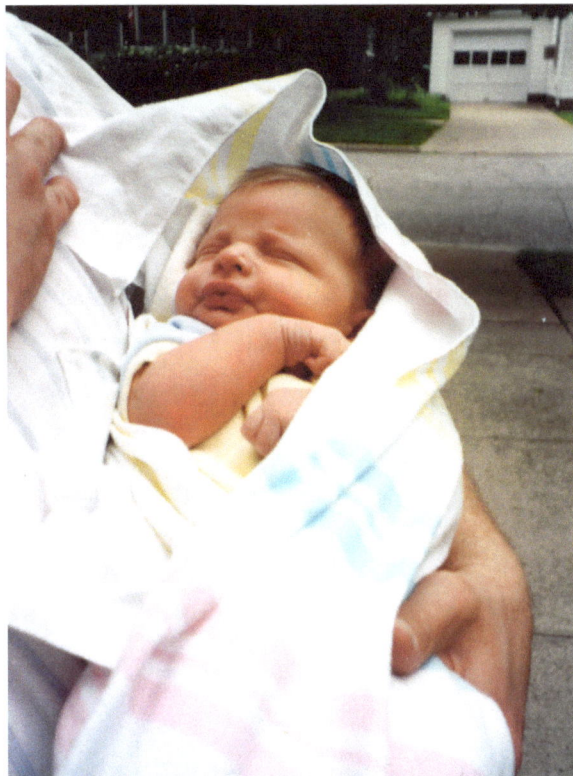

The grandmother and Martha Jane and I stayed one more night in the big brick house. Unknown to us at the time, something special was happening in the neighborhood. A baby boy was born that night to the family in the little house perched on the hill behind the brick house.

The only furniture left in the house was an old daybed and a folding lawn chair. The grandmother slept on the daybed; Martha Jane's bed was a pile of quilts and a sleeping bag on the floor. During that last night she woke me, reaching out across the bare floor to touch my sturdy green form. I read her thoughts in the quiet night air.

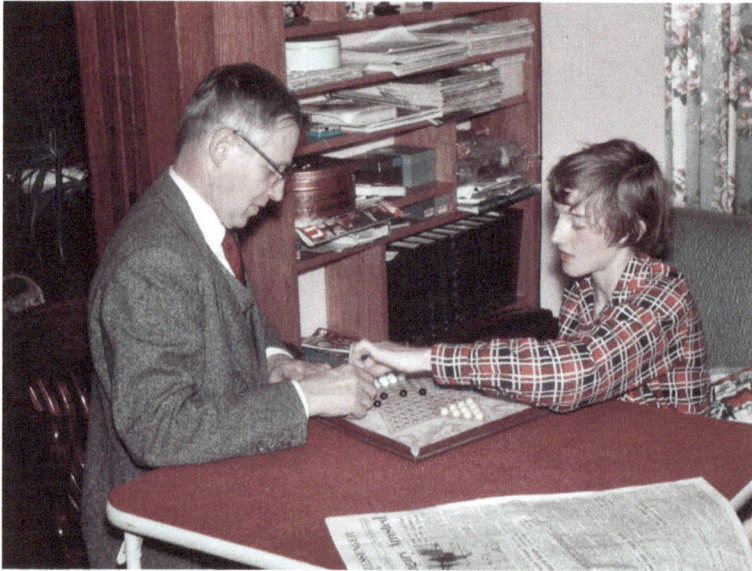

Bittersweet

Her sadness was for the empty house, the grandmother who would miss the wildflowers, the bur oaks, and the wrens. Her thoughts were a kaleidoscope of sights and sounds spanning nearly five decades: the "houses" fashioned in the lilac bushes, made-up games of "Eighteen Wheeler Hopscotch" and "Adios" and the Russian olive trees at the dead end, with thick curved welcoming branches just right for sitting. She remembered waking up summer mornings on the sleeping porch, green-golden light flooding in through a screen of Virginia Creeper. Her thoughts ran to the reading platform that she had built as a young teenag-

er high up in the elm in the front yard. She remembered the games played on the card table in the den: Authors, Parcheesi, Dominoes, and Chinese Checkers.

I saw what she saw in her mind, the cardinals and chickadees, juncoes and nuthatches, and the great fat fox squirrels who feasted at the feeder outside the den window. She saw the path leading from the Russian olive trees down into the ravine, that path forbidden to the children except for the rare forays in the spring to the two places where wild asparagus grew. She thought of the chubby, blue ceramic cookie jar man waiting for the crisp sugar cookies in shapes of dogs and camels, stars, and bells. Seasons swirled in her mind. She saw the grandmother kneeling to tend the bluebells, hepatica, jack-in-the-pulpits, lilies of the valley, and Dutchman's breeches.

Martha Jane sighed as she lightly touched my triangular plates there in the silent night on the bare oak floor of the living room.

Was it silly for a grown woman to be this sad at the thought of saying good-bye to a papier-mâché dinosaur? I knew that it was not. And I knew why. I had become more than a paper toy crafted years ago by a child's hands. I had become a symbol. I represented all that had happened within the walls of the old brick house over five decades. There was change in the air. It had to do with the grandmother in her nineties finishing the final chapter of her family's life in this house and stepping bravely on to a new living place with new people. It had to do with new life, the baby boy in the little house perched on the edge of the hill. It had to do with those who were yesterday's children becoming today's parents and tomorrow's grandparents. And somehow it had to do with me.

I suppose I was a reminder of the magic of moonlit summer nights flickering with fireflies, of church bells ringing at midnight on snowy Christmas Eves, of lean, brown-limbed children in tree houses, and hot dogs cooked on sticks over a campfire and eaten on red and green plastic tableware. Within me were the joyful hugs of hello and the tears of goodbye, the letting go of pet crows and

dogs and grandfathers and neighbors when their moments of final departure came, and the strength to stand tall and nurture the new children and hamsters and puppies that life would present.

Final Goodbye

Martha Jane woke me to talk. I had been expecting this. We each knew what the other was thinking, and we knew that we agreed. Still it was hard. Early on we had both assumed that I would go north in the big truck. Certainly I was never destined for the porch sale, the dump or Goodwill. Yet something was definitely changing in me since leaving the dark safety of my closet shelf. My thick green skin was becoming increasingly brittle; old wounds were daily more painful. Every day new cracks appeared in my

beautiful but fading red, green and white triangular plates. My shiny yellow marble eyes were as bright as ever, but often I was too tired to investigate what I saw.

I would return to the forest primeval. The rightness of this plan had occurred to both of us. After all, I was so biodegradable! My stiff limbs and joints would soften through contact with the earth. Eventually I would be able to lie down, a pleasure not yet known to me. Those rolled-up stiff pages of the *Fort Dodge Messenger* chronicling events in Iowa, circa 1952, would merge again with the earth from whence they came. (Whence! What a wonderful overlooked word! Remember my pointing out that I had quite a capacity for understanding? Dinosaur Pulitzer Prize for vocabulary appreciation, perhaps?) Earth to trees to paper to earth. My water soluble paint would harm neither fauna nor flora. How much better that I stand guard awhile longer over the memories of this hill and

house and family, until gradually coming to rest and being one with the earth, than to end up on some other closet shelf until the inevitable accumulation of cracks and tears, fadings, and peelings sent me to a landfill.

The following day before driving across the river to settle the grandmother in her new apartment at Friendship Haven, Martha Jane gently picked me up and headed down the hill at the dead end and into the woods. If she felt a little strange talking to a papier-mâché dinosaur, she didn't show it, and besides, there was no one to hear. She said I would know sun and rain, snow and sleet, and the heat and bitter cold of Iowa seasons. I would know the company of squirrels, chipmunks, mice, and perhaps an occasional fox. Dignity in the natural peace of the forest would be mine to the end.

I told her not to come back to visit me, at least not before many years had passed. Nature needed time to welcome me. Martha Jane understood. She said she remembered a story, something about a pilot stranded in the Sahara and a little boy and a snake. It was best to let go and not look back. Her tears fell as we parted and would again later when she tried to write all this down. I couldn't spare her that. One manages as best one can the affairs of one's heart.

A few times early on, the grandmother came back from the retirement home to check on the house before it sold and to see how I was doing. She called my name in greeting from the top of the hill but did not try to come see me. She understood.

Remember I told you I could recite all those old children's stories? When I think of Martha Jane, I remember Christopher Robin affectionately referring to Pooh as "silly old bear!" Martha Jane did tend to be a bit emotional over the good old days of her childhood. We may all yearn for the best we have known in life, yet life moves us along to new chapters. You know, I did love her, silly old girl!

Months passed. I grew tired. My stiff old joints softened and I was able to lie down, something that had been but a dim dream all those years on the closet shelf. Oh, could there be anything more blissful?

I slept more and more and finally slipped away into the earth one warm September night but not before startling a few robins and thrushes and earning the trust of rabbits and one resident chipmunk.

And now let's imagine ...

Seven years pass.

A young boy from the little house perched on the hill behind the brick house
comes running home from his morning's adventures as an intrepid explorer.
"Look what I found, Mom!"
He opens his small fist to reveal two slightly smudged yellow marbles,
each with one black dot.

Heartfelt appreciation to

∽ Joan Bratley and Nancy Newman who listened
to the idea of Steggy as we sat in front of the fire at the
Bark Point a-frame 30 years ago;

∽ Terri Wagner who read and reread the story, asking
questions, and offering encouragement and insight;

∽ Parker Sterling, for her wise editing and a nudge
to do something with the story;

∽ Ros Nelson of Little Big Bay Publishing with whom
it has been a joy and great fun to work, as she
encouraged, tweaked, and inspired confidence with
professional excellence;

∽ Hank, Molly and Ethan who were there
and who remember;

∽ and to McKenna, Mallory, Ria and Taylor who have
created new and wonderful memories
of childhood for all of us.